THE
MANIFESTATION
COLOURING BOOK

First published in Great Britain in 2022 by
Michael O'Mara Books Limited
9 Lion Yard
Tremadoc Road
London SW4 7NQ

A CIP catalogue record for this book is available from the British Library.

Papers used by Michael O'Mara Books Limited are natural, recyclable products made from wood grown in sustainable forests. The manufacturing processes conform to the environmental regulations of the country of origin.

ISBN: 978-1- 78929-473-6 in paperback print format

1 2 3 4 5 6 7 8 9 10

Designed by Ana Bjezancevic

Printed and bound in China

www.mombooks.com

THE MANIFESTATION COLOURING BOOK

BRING YOUR GOALS TO LIFE WITH CREATIVE IMAGINATION

Gill Thackray

Illustrated by Pimlada Phuapradit

Michael O'Mara Books Limited

Introduction

Manifesting is a process. When you manifest you create a specific vision that you want to bring into your physical reality, but it's so much more than merely picturing something in your mind's eye. By intentionally shifting your mindset to match your soul's true journey, you'll begin to call in the law of attraction. It takes focus, planning, accountability and trust in the process.

Our thoughts, feelings, words and beliefs hold their own unique vibration and power. We need to use them consciously and consistently. Like attracts like. Become focused. When we manifest with gratitude and joy we intentionally cultivate the energy that we want to attract because, ultimately, what we think, we become.

This formula is your roadmap to total transformation,
for anything that you dream of changing.

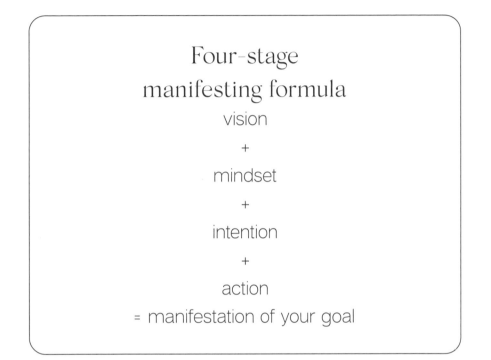

Four-stage manifesting formula

vision

+

mindset

+

intention

+

action

= manifestation of your goal

Manifesting is a way of intentionally working with universal
laws to fulfil your potential.

You can manifest in any area of your life. Purpose, health,
love, relationships, being kinder, making a difference in the
world, abundance, changing yourself or healing the planet.
The choice is yours.

As you begin to manifest, you'll notice signs, messages and
positive coincidences appearing in your life exactly when
you need them. Watch them unfold. The first step of your
journey starts today.

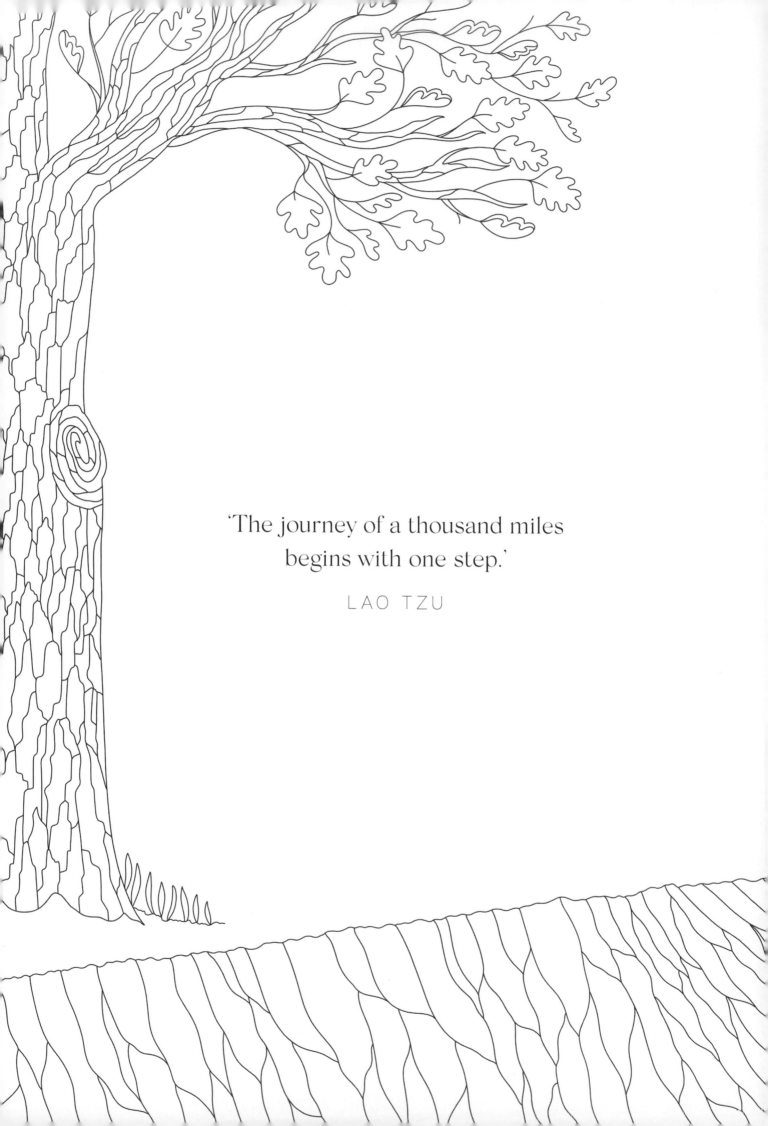

'The journey of a thousand miles
begins with one step.'

LAO TZU

Grounding

When you ground, you are connecting with the
earth, creating a calm and centred platform from
which to manifest. Ground yourself by imagining
roots spreading out from your feet, deep down into
the soft, moist soil, connecting with Mother Earth.

The Law
of Attraction

What we think, we become. The things we focus on,
we move towards. What values and energy are you
bringing into the world? Elevate your thinking. Plant
the seeds of your future success with your thoughts.
Connect to your pure essence and refine the energy
that you send out into the universe.

'Luck is what happens when
preparation meets opportunity.'

SENECA

Conch Shells

In India, China and Southeast Asia, conch shells are regarded as spiritual symbols of great mystery and power. In Buddhism, it is one of eight auspicious symbols, known as the Ashtamangala. Partner with the magic of the conch and the mystery of the universe as you manifest your new future.

Say Goodbye to your Comfort Zone

Manifesting means stepping out of your comfort zone. Grow and stretch beyond that safe place. What served you in getting to this point won't support you in moving forwards. Begin today.

'Don't wait.
The time will never be "just right."'

NAPOLEON HILL

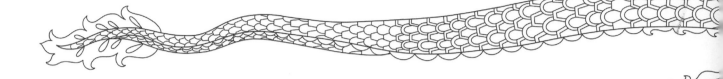

Dragons

In Southeast Asia, dragons are recognized as symbols of power. These mythical creatures embody the fierceness and magnificence of potential. Step into your own personal power as you begin to manifest.

Mountain Manifesting

It's time to soar beyond the mountains that you've only dared to dream of up until this point. When you set your manifesting intentions, aim for the stars; don't limit yourself. Do the thing that scares you.

Intentions and Goals

Intentions and goals connect you with the universal
power within you and around you, helping you
to focus and direct your energy. Remember,
you are the one who creates your reality, so
devote time to re-imagining a world that reflects
your deepest wishes. Awaken your imagination.
Connect with your power.

'Reality is an illusion,
albeit a persistent one.'

EINSTEIN

Believe

The people who create change in their lives believe that it's possible. Activate your intentions by dreaming them into existence. Ignite those dreams by taking action. Your intentions and goals are a framework: your roadmap to complete transformation. Believe in yourself.

Om

When spoken or chanted, Om (pronounced 'Aum')
is regarded as the entire universe in one single sound.
Known as the mystic syllable, the curves and waves
of the Om symbol represent your internal state.
Lean into your inner world, bringing your mind,
body and spirit into balance with this sacred symbol
of the universe. Use it to chant, meditate or pray
as you connect more deeply with what you want
to manifest in the world.

Is it Magic?

Manifesting is a magical combination of vision, action
and a willingness to co-create alongside the universe.
You go beyond dreaming when you manifest.
A mysterious alchemy happens when these
elements are lined up together.

Creating Positive Connections

As humans, we all have a need for connection. Positive connections protect us against negative energies such as anxiety, fear and envy. Create your own supportive, nourishing ecosystem of positivity. Surround yourself with positive connections, people, places and things.

'Set your life on fire.
Seek those who fan your flames.'

RUMI

Nature Ally

Nature is the supreme guide. The natural world teaches us about the cycles of life, change, resilience and effortless abundance. Traditionally, nature allies appear in your life to guide and protect you. Step outside, slow down and connect with the spirit of your nature ally. Build a relationship with them, listening out for the messages they have for you.

The Four Direction Archetypes

The four cardinal directions, or four winds as they are sometimes known, are represented in multiple spiritual traditions. You'll find reference to them in ancient mythology from the druids, Africa, Indian yogis and shamans in the Americas. Each cardinal direction has a specific archetype along with an element of earth, air, fire, or water. Work with the directions to connect with and honour nature as you manifest. She's an amazing teacher.

Serpent

Serpent is the archetype of the South. She teaches us
that our future is not determined by our past. Just as
Serpent sheds her skin, we can shed our past along
with everything else we no longer need as
we embark on our transformative journey.

Jaguar

Jaguar, archetype of the West, helps us to move past anxiety and fear. Great Jaguar will help you to see in the darkness, to find your way. She'll help you to fearlessly explore your unconscious, uncovering the areas that you need to work on to come into alignment with universal energy.

Hummingbird

Archetype of the North, Hummingbird will teach you
to appreciate the beauty that already exists in your life.
Call on Hummingbird to work with you in creating
a life filled with nectar.

Eagle

The archetype of the East, Eagle soars from the
direction of the rising sun. Fly high on the wind with
Eagle, above rivers and mountains to gain perspective
on what you want to be part of changing in the world.

Full Moon

When the moon, sun and earth are aligned it creates a full moon. This powerful alignment and lunar peak are the perfect time to walk in rhythm with nature. Manifest new desires and say goodbye to what no longer serves you. Compost it and give it back to the earth to transmute. Call into being a life that you have deliberately designed with positive intention.

The Palingenesis Cycle

The Palingenesis cycle represents rebirth, new life and a new path. It consists of galaxies, stars, suns and moons. Following the contours of the cosmos, it connects your new manifesting path with the universe. Don't like what you see? Change it. It's time to re-create as you examine every single aspect of your life. You hold the universe in your hands.

Bamboo

In Chinese culture, bamboo symbolizes a long life
filled with luck, prosperity, longevity and success.
In Feng shui, the ancient art of harmonizing energy
or *qi*, lucky bamboo attracts positive energy,
balancing the elements around you. To align
the energies in your environment, place lucky
bamboo in the eastern part of your living space.

Soul Level Manifesting

Transcend the expectations of others and the pressure of what you think you *should* want. What does your soul ache for? Cut through the noise: what is your heart whispering to you? It doesn't have to conform to what society says you should want. You're not here to perform for anyone else or pursue their dreams instead of your own. You're unique. Listen to your soul.

'Fortune and love favour the brave.'

OVID

Laughing Buddha

The laughing Buddha, or Budai in Chinese, is regarded as an incarnation of the Bodhisattva Maitreya. A symbol of happiness, positive energies and joy, he attracts prosperity wherever he goes. Align your mood and your vibration with his abundant, uplifting energy.

The Myth of Perfection

Stop striving for 'perfect'. It doesn't exist. It's an invitation to block yourself with imposter syndrome and thoughts about how undeserving you are. Embrace and honour what you want to craft at your soul level, building a life of abundance that flows from awe and joy.

'My heart is at ease knowing that what was meant for me will never miss me, and that what misses me was never meant for me.'

IMAM AL-SHAFI'I

Changing the World One Manifestation at a Time

Is manifesting about accumulating stuff? No. If your
soul is telling you that something in the collective
chaos needs to change, listen to it. Any thought that
keeps tugging at you, telling you that something
isn't right, is there for a reason. It wants you (yes,
you) to tackle it head on. Maybe it's time for a
paradigm shift, a change in global consciousness,
or you want to be a loving presence, a catalyst
for a more compassionate community. Now
is the time to transcend old models. Take your
manifesting to the highest level and heal the world.

'Be a lamp, or a lifeboat, or a ladder.
Help someone's soul heal.
Walk out of your house like a shepherd.'

RUMI

Step into
Your Power

Take back your power from that little voice that falsely tells you that you're not good enough, smart enough, or loveable enough. Face your fear. Remember that the things you want are on the other side of that fear and doubt. Calibrate your perception. Tell yourself that success is already on the way. Create the conditions for transformation. Learn to accept a compliment with grace. Say 'thank you' when someone says 'well done' or tells you how much they appreciate you. Step into your power, honouring your highest self. Witness your power unfolding as those around you will take their cue from you.

'What we are today comes from our thoughts of yesterday, and our present thoughts build our life of tomorrow. Our life is the creation of our mind.'

GAUTAMA BUDDHA

Connect with your Inner Wisdom

Lean in and listen to your wisdom. Step into stillness. What does it tell you? What do you need right here, right now as you manifest transformation? Let your intuition be your compass. It absolutely knows exactly what you need. Trust in your source energy, your inner guide.

'Small opportunities are often the beginning of great enterprises.'

SUN TZU

Elephant

In cultures around the globe, the majestic elephant is a symbol of power, wisdom, luck, love, fertility and longevity. Embody the characteristics, power and sheer magnificence of Elephant as you manifest.

Unlearn 'I'll be happy when . . .'

Don't wait for things to come to you before you feel happy. Embody your future self now. Being the best version of yourself begins the minute you start manifesting. Make a clear decision to manifest the right energetic space into being. Be happy today. Don't wait until you've got everything on your manifesting list. Unlearn the habit of 'I'll be happy when . . .'

'Stop acting so small.
You are the universe in ecstatic motion.'

RUMI

Morning
Manifesting

The dawn of each morning is a daily manifesting
opportunity to reset and restart as you rise.
Approach your big sky manifesting goals
with energy and enthusiasm.

'He who every morning plans the
transactions of the day, and follows that plan,
carries a thread that will guide him through
the labyrinth of the most busy life.'

VICTOR HUGO

Bedtime
Manifesting Ritual

As the sun sets and the moon rises, a bedtime manifesting ritual is an opportunity to review your day. Rituals allow us to embody the concept of conscious living. The end of the day is a rich opportunity for a reset. To remind yourself of what you've learned along with how you can use it to support yourself tomorrow. Don't forget to congratulate yourself: you're one day closer to achieving your dreams.

'Great acts are made up of small deeds.'

LAO TZU

Surfing the Hero's Journey

You're committing to transformation when you manifest. Realigning your core values with how you live your life. You've chosen to surf the archetypal hero's journey. You might meet resistance on the way. Others might feel threatened when you shake things up as you stretch and grow. That's OK. Send them love and light and move on. The path might not be smooth but connecting to your true essence will support you.

Acorns

In ancient Norse culture, the acorn represented
protection. It was believed by the Vikings that oak
trees drew lightning towards their trunks, deflecting
the anger of Thor away from communities. In cultures
throughout the world, acorns represent perseverance,
rebirth, the cycle of life, hope and growth. Focus
on this emblem of potential as you craft your
manifesting goals.

'Great oaks from little acorns grow.'

FOURTEENTH CENTURY PROVERB

Divine Timing

When you walk a manifesting path it's easy to want it all – now. Let go of the timetable that you have in your head. We don't know what's coming or when. The universe has its own schedule. It will bring us what we need at the perfect divine moment, and not a minute too soon. Surrender to possibility. Remain open to the gifts as they unfold and let go. Release your expectations and dwell in a place of trust. It's time to walk hand in hand with the universe.

'The two most powerful warriors are patience and time.'

LEO TOLSTOY

Mandala

Representing the universe, wholeness and self-unity, mandalas are used in many spiritual traditions around the globe. Creating a mandala is a sacred rite that manifests a unique and beautiful energy. Meditate on what you wish to manifest as you bring your dream into the physical realm. Wisdom reveals itself naturally when you sit in that beautiful space of inner knowing and contemplation. Trust in the unseen.

Energy Boost

As you embark on your journey, you're going to
need fuel in your tank. Low energy can create an
imbalance, leading to unnecessary challenges.
Monitor your energetic patterns. Is it positive and
energizing or heavy and depleting? Bring your
body, mind and energy into balance. Feed yourself
with a daily diet of things that nourish you at soul
level in order to express your highest self. Allow it
to permeate every cell in your body, carrying that
energetic renewal to every organ. Whether it's
soothing music, moving poetry or incredible art,
surround yourself with life-affirming beauty.

The Double
Fish Symbol

The auspicious double fish symbol can be found
around the world. Representing abundance, wealth
and good fortune, use this image to connect with the
law of attraction on your personal manifesting journey.

Meditate on Manifesting

Meditation supports your physical and mental wellbeing. It will support your immune system, enable you to focus on your goals and help you to manage stress when things don't go to plan. Focusing on colouring mindfully creates a powerful synchronicity, relaxing you and readying you spiritually for action.

'Every great dream begins with a dreamer. Always remember, you have within you the strength, the patience, and the passion to reach for the stars to change the world.'

HARRIET TUBMAN

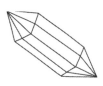

Manifesting
with Chakras

Your chakras are a gateway, internal energetic centres, connecting you to universal energy. An imbalance in our chakras informs us that we're out of alignment with universal energy. If there's stagnant energy, or *qi*, in your chakras you'll notice that you're getting stuck somewhere in your manifesting journey. Clearing your chakras raises your vibrational energy and removes those blocks.

The Wheel
of the Year

This ancient cycle honours and celebrates nature's cycle. Each segment of the wheel represents a festival. Known as the eight sabbats, they correspond with the earth's natural rhythm. When is the best time to plan your day? Today. Planning and goal setting isn't just for the new year. Align your journey with the wheel to plot your manifesting journey, synchronizing the energy of the universe and the flow of these powerful seasonal cycles.

Samhain (Hallowe'en)

Samhain, the beginning and end of the calendar, is the Celtic new year. Traditionally this is the time when the veil between our world and non-ordinary reality is at its thinnest. This is a time to connect with your inner wisdom and perform manifesting rituals as you honour the ancient Celtic cycle.

Winter Solstice (Yule)

The stillness of winter provides a place to
reflect on your progress. Review what you've
achieved, your lessons and how you've grown.
Contemplate where you want to go next on your
manifesting journey. Ask yourself: what next?

Imbolc (Candlemas)

The worst of winter has passed, and the first signs of
spring are beginning to emerge. It's time to cultivate
new dreams and new beginnings. Now is the time
to focus on the seeds that you wish to sow. Set your
intentions and goals ready for the coming year.
Write them down. Studies have shown how just
putting pen to paper makes it more likely that
you'll achieve your goals.

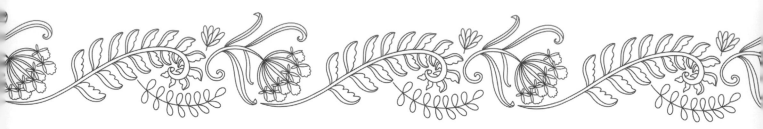

Spring Equinox (Ostara)

The spring equinox brings a balance of dark and light. This phase of new life provides an opportunity to think about what you can let go of and ask yourself, 'Where do I want to grow?' Say goodbye (and thank you) to the old patterns, habits and thoughts that brought you here but are now no longer necessary. Focus on your new goals and take steps to bring them into your external reality. Harness the energy of spring.

Beltane (May Eve)

Beltane, meaning 'bright fire', is the first day of summer, a time of abundance and a celebration of life. This is a time to really focus all of your creative energy on your dreams, intentions and goals.

Summer Solstice (Litha)

This festival marks the longest day, the apex of the year. Recognize what you've achieved. Pause and stand still for a moment on your journey, grounding yourself in the expansiveness of summer light.

Lughnasadh (Lammas)

Known as the grain festival, this is the time of harvest.
Extend gratitude and give thanks for the lessons
and achievements you've reaped on your
manifesting journey.

Autumn Equinox (Mabon)

Mabon, the final fire festival, marks the time when we begin to move towards shorter days as the light recedes and the days draw in. Reflect on your achievements and what still needs to be accomplished before winter approaches. Lean into your inner landscape as you prepare to replenish and regenerate in the darkness of Yule until Imbolc.

Amplifying Positive Experiences

Rewire your brain by teaching yourself to focus on the positive experiences that occur on your manifesting journey. When you amplify the positives in your life, the universe will multiply them. When something good happens, immerse yourself in it.

'Do not feel lonely,
the entire universe is inside you.'

RUMI

Four Leaf Clover

In ancient Celtic folklore, the four-leaf clover symbolizes good luck. In Irish folk tradition, the clover represents faith, love, protection and hope in addition to luck. Connect with the spirit of clover for protection and good fortune as you manifest.

Manifesting with the Elements

Tap into the universal energy that is all around you. For millennia, wisdom traditions have recognized the power of nature. Join forces with the immense energy of the elements, coming into balance with their energetic flow.

'If we could see the miracle of a single flower clearly, our whole life would change.'

BUDDHA

Manifesting with Air

Send your manifesting intentions out on the breeze
to be carried to the four corners of the earth and
see what returns. Spread your wings, open up
and access the vital energy of this element.

Manifesting with Water

Move with the power and rhythm of the ocean.
Dance with the waves. Allow the current to stir your
heart, setting you free from old limits as you discover
your true direction.

'You are not a drop in the ocean.
You are the entire ocean, in a drop.'

RUMI

Manifesting with Fire

When your journey requires intense energy, match
your vibration with the element of fire. Burn through
obstacles and doubt with the sacred flames.

Manifesting with Earth

Use the energy of rocks or mountains to ground
yourself when doubt creeps into your mind and
you need to steady yourself.

Manifesting Mantras

Used around the world for centuries, reciting a mantra
is a way of communicating with the universe at a
specific vibrational level. Whether it's a sound, a word
or a sentence, make it magical and positive to align
your inner vibration with all that you want to manifest
outwardly in the world.

Manifesting Abundance

The foundations of an abundant life lie within your mindset. You consciously create abundance by believing that it's possible. Become super conscious about how you're using your thoughts and what you believe is possible. Bring your attention to your beliefs. Notice the messages that have been unconsciously hardwired into your belief system and reprogram them.

Connecting with your Inner Goddess

The Divine Feminine is a powerful spiritual ally. She is known by many names: Madonna, Black Madonna, Ala, Pacha-mama, Spider Grandmother, Shakti or Gaia. She is the Great Mother, the source of all creation. Connect with this powerful Goddess energy as you birth your new life. Now is the time to embrace your inner Goddess, aligning with your highest path.

Shooting Stars

Shooting stars have long been believed
to be an auspicious portent of change.
Representing luck, ambition and purity, they are
a vehicle of positivity. Place your manifesting
wishes upon this magical symbol.

'It does not matter how slowly you go as long
as you do not stop.'

CONFUCIUS

About the Author

Gill Thackray is a performance psychologist, lecturer, author and coach, helping clients globally to create conscious transformation and positive change. She has lived and worked with indigenous communities around the world, in Southeast Asia and China, studying the science of healing and ancient wisdom traditions. Gill is a trained shamanic practitioner, currently undertaking PhD research into indigenous healing practices and eco-psychology. She can be found at www.planetpositivechange.com

Her books include *The Mindfulness Coach*, *The Positivity Coach*, *How to Manifest* and *The Manifestation Journal*, all published by Michael O'Mara Books.